Social
Crypto Libertarianism
("Not Capital")

Victor Porton

2020

Abstract

The book describes the new political (economical) ideology under the contingent name *social crypto libertarianism* or *left crypto libertarianism* (Note that it is not social, not left, and not libertarianism, I call it so for lack of more suitable words.) and the practical steps of how to implant this concept into modern economy. You are offered to participate in the experiment volunteering or for a reward.

Table of Contents

License

You can post your own articles related to this book at https://en.wikiversity.org/wiki/Social_Crypto_Libertarianism

This book is licensed under Creative Commons Attribution-ShareAlike License 3.0:

You are free to:

- Share — copy and redistribute the material in any medium or format

- Adapt — remix, transform, and build upon the material

- for any purpose, even commercially.

This license is acceptable for Free Cultural Works.

The licensor cannot revoke these freedoms as long as you follow the license terms.

Under the following terms:

- Attribution — You must give appropriate credit, provide a link to the license, and indicate if changes were made. You may do so in any reasonable manner, but not in any way that suggests the licensor endorses you or your use.

- ShareAlike — If you remix, transform, or build upon the material, you must distribute your contributions under the same license as the original.

No additional restrictions — You may not apply legal terms or technological measures that legally restrict others from doing anything the license permits.

Introduction

Social crypto libertarianism or *left crypto libertarianism* is a new political (economical) ideology originating from Victor Porton.

Social crypto libertarianism is a contingent slogan. It is not social, not left, and not libertarianism. There are probably just no better words to describe it in modern English.

This book describes the ideology and the scholarly experiment to implant social crypto libertarianism into the modern society. The experiment is both scientific (to check if these ideas work in practice) and applied (to try to enhance world economy). The radical idea of social crypto libertarianism is that it can replace capitalism as the dominating world economical mode (while preserving free market).

In this book I also propose you a paid work and a business that I can create for you!

The definition

(The definition has been changed compared to the original version of this text: Added the thing about prediction markets.)

Social crypto libertarianism has the following defining properties:

- More or less libertarian political system (with the main defining property being degrading importance and role of state). However, accordingly Victor Porton, it could be implanted in the near future inside the existing political and economical system.

- Emphasis on importance of social good, charity, equity (but, in general, not equality).

- Exchange of values based on an universal global payment system (crypto).

- Support of social (and individual) good by minting crypto (that is producing quantities of money "out of nothing", inflation).

- Making some of important economical decisions in two ways:

  - by the traditional free market based capitalistic process;

  - based on:

    - voting rather than directly by the free market. (Particularly, voting committees (or "reward courts") could mint crypto to support charity.)

      - The right to everyone to create or support voting committees that make economical decisions.

    - free market of prediction tokens. (Particularly, prediction tokens could be rewarded in the case if the prediction comes true with minted tokens, here the line between business and charity is blurred.)

The results

Victor Porton expects the following effects of implanting the social crypto libertarianism:

- enhanced support of charity

- UBI

- increased efficiency of the economy (better support of open source, science, inventions, and other social good projects, etc.)

- increased equity

- increased equality among poorer layers of the society

- increased inequality among the most rich, appearance of trillionaires of people producing social good (such as possibly Linus Torvalds, Greta Thunberg, me for both this project and my math research)

- better providing compensation to victims

Advantages and disadvantages of social crypto libertarian economy

There are the following advantages:

- In existing economy charities have limited funds to support projects and usually need to choose between several important projects. But minting charity tokens idea allows to allocate unlimited amounts of funding (in fact limited by world resources available or reasonable for a particular part of economy). So charity will thrive.

- Good deeds (e.g. writing an open source software) are rewarded.

- A way to possibly reverse the climate change and other environmental projects as we can mint tokens for ecological projects.

- Funding global projects independently of the country and region of originating.

Disadvantages:

- Proposed voting mechanisms are more subjective than capitalistic free market, they may lead to corruption in committees. (So prediction market approach (see below) seems even more promising.)

Theory of the Revolution

The experiment is not enough theoretically founded, because even existing crypto economy is yet not well understood by the economical science (can you predict the rate of BitCoin?)

What is money? Early economists thought it is an expression of material goods, like an obligation for gold. Now in crypto epoch we know that money can exist without material goods backing them. Money is a number that can be transferred safely between accounts.

The foundation of the Victor Porton's hypothesis is the following: The value of BitCoin and some other cryptocurrencies is founded on their difficulty to obtain. The crypto produced by the experiment would be also hard to obtain because it is deemed hard enough to persuade a committee to vote for allocating crypto to you or a prediction market to trade in your gain. So by the supposed analogy the minted cryptocurrencies will have significant value despite of not being backed, just like BitCoin.

We don't know the limits of the value of such minted cryptocurrencies, but it seems reasonable to assume that it is bounded above by the approximate worth of the financed (charity and other) projects.

Multi-currency system

The modern economy is single-currency. Well, there is its own currency in many of countries, but they are almost the same currency in different measures, as they can be exchanged to each other back-and-forth.

This system is far too primitive for the modern world where different kinds of values exist. Every kind of value needs its own currency. For example, there are:

- material goods

- rights (legal rights, digital rights, freedom of be heard, etc.)

- intellectual properties

Each of them needs its own currency kind.

We need many currencies to value many kinds of good deeds. We cannot know the exchange rate of different kinds of good in advance, so it is up to free market to decide.

Goods vs Rights and Business vs Nonprofit

To be able to analyze complex things of the real world, we need to split all resources of our civilization into two categories: goods and rights.

Characteristics of goods:

- Goods cost money to produce every item.

- Goods can be owned by a business, usually in potentially unlimited quantities.

- Goods can be moved between persons and/or organizations.

Characteristics of rights:

- Rights should belong to everybody.

- Rights are not a part of the industrial economy.

- Rights are often tied to an individual human or an individual organization and are often not transferable.

- It is hard to impossible or impractical to sell rights.

There is no exact border between goods and rights: Is bread a good or right? It costs money to produce, it can be owned by a business in unlimited quantities, it is a part of the industry (including agriculture), but it should belong to everybody.

My main claim of this section: Rights should be free!

These things are to be counted rights, not goods. It is a middle-age madness when a state takes money to open a business or to provide an ID card. [1]

Goods are usually produced and sold by a business. Business is relatively good in producing goods. We learned that market economy is the best known method we have experienced to produce goods, because as we know socialism mostly failed.

But it is madness when rights are trusted to a business to be sold for money. It is even a greater madness if a state sells rights for it as if it would not have tax and inflation. It is like a billionaire stealing a cent from a beggar (that writes a free software for his business) because he wants to make his business more effective.

Even businesses understand they need to provide free services or free trials to be more effective. The state authorities need psychiatrists: they sell rights for money.

Why rights are so important? Because they are like 1000 times more effective than goods today. The number 1000 times estimated from expenses and advantages of a particular project, the Linux project:

"In 2008 the value of developing a Linux distribution was worth $10.8 billion." [2] But "only Red Hat Enterprise Linux to Impact $10 Trillion of Global Business Revenues in 2019" [3]. Linux impact is many tens trillions of dollars.

We see about 1000 fold or much more impact of a nonprofit project. It is partly because Linux is more like a right than a good, and because it is free.

We see here an example of a right partly developed by a nonprofit (Linux Foundation). Here we switch to the next topic: goods are associated with business, rights are associated with state and nonprofit.

As I said, business is relatively good (I mean better than socialism) in producing goods. Business sometimes produces rights (often bearing heavy burden of expenses to produce them with only a little or no benefit back for the company). But the natural order of things is when rights are produced by nonprofit (or by state, which is somehow like a big nonprofit concerning its citizens).

If the natural order breaks and rights are not produced or distributed for free, we have such problems as:

- People in poverty.

- Economic recession or stagnation.

- Unjust world.

- Need to choose to produce a good/right or to distribute it. It is often not enough to money/time/resources to do both.

- Failed important projects.

- Other.

Scientists do not receive reward for the work they do. Journalists live mostly on as if their work would be so unimportant to deliver them only a little share of their job benefits. Free software authors are sometimes poor and have no money to advertise their products and to improve them. Etc. This is partly from not understanding by the establishment the difference between goods and rights, they tend to think that rights are also a part of market economy and to be sold for money or just ignored if they can't be sold, what is very wrong.

The more world economy and technology develops, the more important rights become (for example, because software needs to be a free right rather than a good to be technically effective). Capitalism with its focus on goods is a too ancient system now. We need an economy that focuses more and more on rights. It is partly because now people have more goods than in the past and so goods lose their importance.

As rights become more important, nonprofits that exist to produce them (yes, the very purpose of nonprofits is to produce and distribute rights) become more important, too.

Capitalism is the business-based economy. We need *nonprofit-based economy*.

The next thing to discuss is human rights. Every human should really have rights. We all know that just to distribute everything for free does not work (especially because people are greedy). But to sell rights for money is a big no. Both variants don't work. What to do? We should distribute some rights (e.g. the right to open a bank account or the right to install an operating system such as Linux for free), we should sell some rights for crypto rather than for money.

The idea (Universal Basic Income or UBI in crypto) is simple: Give every person 1 coin of some specifically created crypto every 0:00 every day. (Need to decide if from the moment of his or her signup in the system or from the moment of the setup of the system or from the moment of his or her birth, etc. I do not know the best way to set the moment this stream of crypto starts to flow.) Then such rights as to have some bread or to be heard in media could be sold for this free crypto rather than to be given for free or to be sold for money. It is a golden middle, better than both extremes to give everyone free money or free goods or to force everybody to pay for rights.

We can also have distinct currencies for different kinds of rights: Spending more on bread should not deprive someone of the right to be heard in media accordingly to widely accepted principles of free speech.

The hardest thing to set this system is to check that one human person does not signup more than once. To do this one needs to set a system to check his personal ID reliably.

Crypto UBI (even already backed with some (however yet small) liquid money) is already implemented in such projects as GoodDollar [4].

Media coverage of a person's ideas should be partly considered a right. It is very bad if a porn star has an advantage over a mathematician in media coverage. It is bad when somebody becomes a moral teacher because he stole more money than others to cover his media expenses. Everybody should have the right not only to say but to be heard. The human crypto could be a partial solution of this problem: We should sell media coverage or ads for this crypto as well, not only for money.

A critique of the traditional libertarianism and anarcho-capitalism

Traditionally libertarians oppose to any authority that is not free market.

My solution includes free courts. It is an authority. A free court is a part of free market, but a court itself isn't a free market (it is a democracy instead). So I am not quite a libertarian.

Traditional libertarianism is defective: Life without courts is incomplete. We need courts. Even "God likes court." (the Bible). Without courts injustice spreads.

My "libertarian" courts are a natural result of evolution of the free market in its modern "crypto" stage. Libertarianism is not ready for crypto and crypto courts, they have nothing to protect you from this good deed :-) To disallow crypto courts one would need unfounded violence and state to accomplish this evil. Libertarians are against such actions. So they can't stop us, even if they want. So, the traditional libertarianism just makes no sense in our crypto smart contract epoch.

However, the prediction market approach seems better than court approach and is more libertarian in spirit.

So, libertarians and anarcho-capitalists are our allies in the sense that we both envision the future world where there is no state or the state is severely limited or weakened.

Why libertarians don't accept our ideas? (as I learned after some communication with Russian libertarians) This is because some of them have a contradictory philosophy: Many of them think that to be a libertarian one needs to be against common good (clearly not true). But their reason to be against common good is that they deem that to be for common good is against common good. Contradiction in their reasoning.

Exiting Software

There exists software for voting whom to mint free crypto tokens to, Crypto Reward Courts.

https://reward.portonvictor.org

Features of this software:

Technologies:

- Ethereum

- Aragon

- ERC-1155 for minted tokens

Voting:

- Any Aragon-based way of voting including:

  - one-person per vote

  - share-percent based voting with either transferable or non-transferable shares

  - different quorums, voting time periods, minimum voters percents

A thing missing is a good ERC-1155 exchange and a gateway between ERC-1155 and ERC-20.

To become a voter you need to:

1. install a crypto browser

2. buy like $10-20 or more of Ether

3. join the Facebook groups as is explained on the site and wait when we gather enough voters and send you further instructions

4. vote through the Web interface, I am available for free tech support

I am improving this software for better "anti-theft" (basically by a multi-level system limiting the amount of tokens transferred between levels) system and support of retiring carbon tokens, see https://github.com/vporton/carbon-flow.

Use of prediction markets

The definition of *prediction market*: "form of financial market, often known as a prediction market, but also going by the name "information market" or "event futures." Analytically, these are markets where participants trade in contracts whose payoff depends on unknown future events." [5]

Prediction markets are implemented in blockchain with such systems as Gnosis [6].

Simply put, the prediction tokens will be guaranty exchanged in the future for some other cryptocurrency only if a prediction comes true.

The author's idea is to combine prediction markets with minted tokens: the reward (*collateral* that is transferred to the prediction contract in the beginning of the race) for making a true prediction is in minted tokens.

This eliminates the need of a voting court that to decide how much tokens to mint. Any pre-minted token could be used as the reward token, because the absolute amount of the minted token obviously does not matter in this case.

The author is going to work on improving Gnosis in the following ways:

- allow to use ERC-1155 tokens as the collateral

- allow any 0..1 number as the weight of the "success" of an outcome rather than simple yes/no (the sum of all such numbers should be 1)

- integration with preminted tokens.

Particular examples of social good prediction markets

- the number of downloads of a given open source software package (need an anti-Sybil protection to avoid manipulations)

- the number of software packages referring to a given open source package

- the above mentioned number adding (probably somehow weighted, it is a topic for further discussion of how to weight it) the number of other packages referring to them directly or indirectly (in the simplest variant the number of all direct and indirect references)

- the number of citations of a given scientific (or other) article

- and (likewise to software packages) counting indirect citations

Self references/citations probably should be excluded (but counted in indirect paths of others' references/citations) to avoid manipulations.

This would allow to pay to a software author or a scientist accordingly to the predicted number of his future references/citations.

It turns open source and science into a business. The line between a business and a charity are blurred this way, so in the future legal system (if any) should be probably no distinction between a business and a charity.

Prediction of prediction markets

The main trouble implementing this idea is the following:

There are no prediction oracles for many important potential prediction markets:

- no reliable public data about the numbers of citations

- no aggregate data about software package interrelations

The best way to solve this problem seems to stimulate the market to create such prediction oracles in the future by providing money to the creators of oracles. (Hey Google, we are hiring you!) This can be done by prediction markets themselves: To kick up the system we initially need to create just one kid of prediction markets, the market of values of prediction markets.

We would have a prediction market for any kind of prediction markets, for example:

- a prediction market for the value of software packages interdepencencies prediction markets

- a prediction market for the value of scientific articles citations prediction markets

Furthermore we would have different prediction markets for different kinds of counting (e.g. taking or not taking into account indirect references, taking or not taking into account creationists' works, etc.)

The good thing about this approach is that it is not too hard to do it: We could value prediction markets of prediction markets just by the usual crypto voting procedure. This voting can be done (among other) in the following ways:

- one person – one vote (needs an anti-Sybil system such as BrightID [7])

- any kind of DAO (e.g. an Aragon [8] DAO)

    - quadratic voting (also needs anti-Sybil) for Aragon is not yet done well enough)

The Mathematical Model

The following is a mathematical model possible to implement in blockchain for stimulating market to implement the author and publisher scoring oracles.

1. Using a special smart contract anybody can claim his account as a science author for purposes of his "salary" accounting.

2. Using a special smart contract anybody can claim his account as a science publisher.

3. Anybody could create (if he has enough money to implement this) an oracle mapping for example scientist's Ethereum address to the number of scientist's citations (accordingly this oracle) and optionally to the publisher(s).

4. Create two prediction markets:

    1. the score of each oracle

    2. the score of each scientist and each publisher by each oracle (so NxM where N is the number of scientists and M is the number of oracles outcomes)

5. Allow anybody to deposit ETH (or a token) to be exchanged for the collateral (after 100+ years, see below). It can be made with something like Uniswap.

6. After 100 years each oracle owner is expected to write the "score" (presumably based on citations counts and licensing/pricing policies) for each scientist (with nonzero results) into the blockchain. He is also expected to score publishers. (A probably simplest way to score publishers is to add scores for all articles for which it is is considered the primary publisher.)

7. During some additional time period the people (or robots) vote resulting scoring each of these oracles 0..1 (with the sum 1) based on how they perceive the "correctness" or "fairness" of its scientists' scores. The voting results are the outcomes of the oracles list predictions.

8. Each oracle receives the collateral proportional to its score.

9. Each scientist receives the collateral proportional to the sum of the products of his score in an oracle to the score of the oracle. (To be retrieved from each oracle funds separately, because potentially there may be many oracles.)

10. Each publisher receives the collateral proportional to its score.

So, we have the prediction markets for scientists, publishers, and oracles, they receive some reward now (not after 100 years).

How to split the collateral into three parts between scientists, publishers, and oracles? It could be done by voting after 100 years with voting results taking the arithmetic averages from each voter. Or we can start voting now and keep it running for 100 years.

We could also pay to reviewers but that's not possible to do fairly as they are anonymous.

I am going to work on this as a blockchain developer.

Requirements to start the experiment and proposed consequences

To start the experiment with reward courts Victor Porton proposes to form a committee of 5 members with equal non-transferable voting rights. Please contact porton@narod.ru if you want to join the experiment. (Victor Porton may probably even pay you some liquid money as stimulation to participate. Moreover, nothing limits you to allocate funds to yourself as a part of the experiment.)

Victor Porton supposes that committees/courts will reproduce by funding more like-minded committees, thus becoming a global phenomenon. The experiment is to check this outcome.

We are to try to measure:

- the distribution of the value of minted tokens produced by the committees

- the distribution of the share of the tokens allocated by the committees to themselves or their members

- the rate of the reproduction of the committee

- the distribution of the quantity of members of a committee, the voting methods used

Proposed rules for the first committee

The committee members can be either volunteer or paid (contact porton@narod.ru if you want to participate). In any case the committee member can vote to allocate funds to themselves to make a business of this work.

The committee consists of 5 individuals.

Areas of the committee

The committee makes decisions on the following issues (each of these four main points has a separate token):

- Rewarding individuals (individuals, registered and unregistered organizations, giving an advantage to individuals and non-profit organizations) on merit in the field:

- charity, giving priority to merit in the field of cryptocurrency philanthropy, primarily merit in "printing" (producing "out of nowhere") cryptocurrencies or tokens for charity purposes.

- Rewarding the same categories of persons for creating socially useful and potentially socially useful open source products.

- Awarding the same categories of persons for measures to reduce the amount of carbon dioxide in the atmosphere in the amount of 1 token per expected ton of carbon dioxide, as well as an equivalent award for other equivalent measures to combat global warming, including (but not limited to) awards for:

- installation of solar panels;

- political and advocacy actions to combat global warming;

- R&D in the field of combating global warming.

- Compensation for under-represented, unrewarded, or poorly rewarded, as well as victims of disasters, setbacks, crimes, unfair laws, etc.

Rewards for charity should be proportional to the intended public benefit (and not just the amount of the donation). Public benefit is understood as the development of society, the not useless complication of the structure of science, technology, education, human relations, or such an alleged benefit in the future.

The committee should award individuals regardless of citizenship, place of registration, nationality, religion, political views (except for cases where political views correlate with merits in these areas), academic and other titles. Notwithstanding the above, the committee should give some priority to the poor, under-represented, unrewarded or under-paid, as well as victims of disasters, failures, crimes, unjust laws, etc., but also reward other categories of persons, guided primarily by merit (except for the last nomination above).

Duties of committee members

Participate and vote on all issues in all meetings of the committee, except for cases involving dismissal from work in accordance with the labor code of the location of the committee member.

Come to a compromise and agreement on controversial issues.

Examine all necessary software sufficiently.

Treat Ethereum secret codes with care, do not transfer them to third parties, when using unsafe operating systems, constantly check for malicious software, and when software security updates appear, install them immediately.

Pay from their own funds all expenses for the work of the committee, including the "gas" of the Ethereum system.

Each new committee member is required to undergo a video interview with Victor Porton and be appointed only in case of a positive decision by Victor Porton.

In the event that a committee member is awarded, put up his own reward for public auction, while prudently postponing a significant part of the reward for the future, based on their assumptions about the growth of its exchange rate.

Work on the committee at least ___ hours per week.

Read this agreement and the rules adopted by the committee.

When deciding to withdraw from the committee, ensure participation in the vote on your replacement.

Do not use the absence of some committee members for any reason to make important decisions bypassing the majority opinion. If the decision is made in this way, it is considered invalid (except for the case when its cancellation is impossible for objective reasons).

In the course of the committee's work, do not mislead anyone on any issue.

Responsibilities of the committee

Carry out permanent work (except for the case when the work was not paid) for rewarding cryptocurrency by voting.

Make fair, effective, intelligent decisions.

Elect the chairman of the committee as necessary.

Pass the "laws" by which the committee acts.

In the event of permanent or prolonged retirement of a committee member from the committee's work process, elect a new committee member to replace him. When electing a new committee member, give preference to volunteers.

Actively search for persons to be awarded.

Convincing potential recipients to receive the award and use it in exchange for liquid funds. Inform the recipients of the award, possible methods of exchange for liquid values, and the need to save a significant part of the award due to the expected increase in its price.

Reward in proportion to the merit, in accordance with the merit assessment by the committee.

Reward committee members on an equal footing with other categories of persons, if committee members have the appropriate merits (including merits for work in the committee). The rewards to the committee members should be modest, that is, they should not collapse the rate of the corresponding token.

To exclude from the committee members those who seriously violate this agreement or the rules adopted by the committee.

As far as the rationality of these actions, make decisions about the categories of projects and actions, which are emphasized in the reward and the search for potential recipients.

The responsibilities of the committee are distributed among the members of the committee by consensus.

Check newly admitted committee members for qualifications and moral qualities. Do not admit those convicted of economic crimes, as well as those who are thoroughly suspected of such, as members of the committee.

Accept for consideration all adequate requests for awards, unless their number exceeds the ability of the committee to consider.

Duties of the chairman to the committee

The chairman of the committee must carefully maintain a separate Facebook page for each court topic in English about all decisions made by the committee, as well as important issues discussed in the committee (if they are not reasonably secret).

Publish to these pages the decisions about the categories of projects and activities that are emphasized in the award and the search for potential recipients.

Maintain and moderate Facebook groups, where everyone can ask for rewarding themselves, or someone else.

The personal story of the author

The author of this book, Victor Porton, finally converted to the Baptist faith when he was 15.

For the reasons outside of the topic of this book, I decided to call myself a sectarian and a religious fanatic, telling it to everybody whenever the topic arouse.

I realized that I am going to the death: If I represent myself to Russian (I am from Russia) people this way, nobody will speak with me, I will be unable to find a job, get a charity support and would just die of hunger. This almost accomplished: I was as thin as a death camp survivor. Several times I fell unable to move because of the hunger. (For example, once I succeed to plead a piece of chocolate from somebody; but when I was going to eat, because of hunger I fell, the chocolate fell near me and I was not able to move anymore to reach the chocolate.)

Believe me or not, but while being 18 years old, a first year university student, between two "lunches" of eating grass on the streets, I discovered a new important math formula. It probably costs a trillion dollars if not more, because it was discovered about 60 years late.

What was killing me was not capitalism (as Russia already was that time). In a socialistic society I would probably have no less chances to die.

I was being killed by the corrupted Elzin's state that illegally sponsored religious propaganda against me.

The state kills, so I am like a libertarian if not anarchist.

I am a trillionaire. You may have the illusion that I am not. But my formulas are worth $trillions.

And what reward have I received from the society for my work? Zero! I was forced to leave the university without any scientific degree because after it I would likely die of hunger. I managed to get a disability pension to be able to survive.

Well, later I changed my religious attitude. Now I am earning some money with freelance programming jobs.

But the state reward system is… which word to use? You understand. It splits the society into castes: having or not having business licenses, having or not having scientific degrees. Your payment is accordingly your caste more than accordingly your work.

We need an independent reward system.

I am a trillionaire. I want to be able to exchange my knowledge for dollars whenever I wish.

Bibliography

1: Victor Porton, The cost of NGO and business registration should be set to zero, , https://barriers.portonvictor.org/2019/05/03/the-cost-of-ngo-and-business-registration-should-be-set-to-zero/
2: The Linux Foundation, Linux Foundation Publishes Study Estimating the Value of Linux, October 22, 2008,
3: Red Hat, Inc., New Research Expects Red Hat Enterprise Linux to Impact $10 Trillion of Global Business Revenues, Employ 900,000 IT Professionals in 2019, May 7, 2019,
4: GoodDollar, GoodDollar: Global UBI on Blockchain, ,
5: Wolfers, Justin, and Eric Zitzewitz, Prediction Markets, 2004
6: Gnosis Ltd., Gnosis, , https://gnosis.io
7: , Universal Proof of Uniqueness, October 17th, 2020, https://www.brightid.org/whitepaper
8: Aragon Association, Aragon, , https://aragon.org

www.ingramcontent.com/pod-product-compliance
Lightning Source LLC
Chambersburg PA
CBHW050806240726
48654CB00008B/652